50 Premium Foreign International Breakfast Dishes

By: Kelly Johnson

Table of Contents

- **Japanese Tamago Kake Gohan** (Egg Over Rice)
- **French Croissant aux Amandes** (Almond Croissant)
- **Mexican Chilaquiles con Huevos**
- **Turkish Menemen** (Spicy Scrambled Eggs with Tomatoes)
- **English Full Breakfast** (Bacon, Eggs, Sausages, Beans)
- **Indian Masala Dosa** (Fermented Rice Crepe with Spiced Potatoes)
- **Spanish Tortilla Española** (Potato and Egg Omelet)
- **German Bauernfrühstück** (Farmer's Breakfast with Potatoes & Eggs)
- **Korean Gyeran Bap** (Egg Rice Bowl with Sesame Oil)
- **Argentine Medialunas con Dulce de Leche** (Sweet Croissants with Caramel)
- **Lebanese Manakish Za'atar** (Flatbread with Thyme & Olive Oil)
- **Russian Syrniki** (Sweet Cheese Pancakes)
- **Chinese Dim Sum Breakfast** (Variety of Steamed Dumplings)
- **Brazilian Pão de Queijo** (Cheese Bread)
- **Moroccan Bissara** (Fava Bean Soup with Olive Oil)
- **Italian Cornetto e Cappuccino** (Pastry with Coffee)
- **Vietnamese Bánh Mì Op La** (Egg and Baguette Sandwich)
- **Dutch Poffertjes** (Mini Pancakes with Butter & Powdered Sugar)
- **Filipino Tapsilog** (Beef, Garlic Rice & Fried Egg)
- **Swedish Gravlax Smörgås** (Cured Salmon on Dark Rye Bread)
- **Greek Bougatsa** (Custard-Filled Pastry with Cinnamon)
- **South African Boerewors and Pap** (Sausage with Maize Porridge)
- **Ethiopian Genfo** (Barley Porridge with Spiced Butter)
- **Persian Kuku Sabzi** (Herb and Egg Frittata)
- **Austrian Kaiserschmarrn** (Caramelized Pancake with Raisins)
- **Thai Jok** (Rice Porridge with Pork and Ginger)
- **Colombian Arepas con Queso** (Cheese-Stuffed Corn Cakes)
- **Danish Wienerbrød** (Layered Pastry with Almond Paste)
- **Polish Racuchy** (Yeast Pancakes with Apples)
- **Hungarian Lángos** (Fried Dough with Sour Cream & Cheese)
- **Finnish Karjalanpiirakka** (Rice-Filled Rye Pastry)
- **Indonesian Bubur Ayam** (Chicken Rice Porridge)
- **Egyptian Ful Medames** (Slow-Cooked Fava Beans with Garlic)
- **Peruvian Tamal con Salsa Criolla** (Corn Dough with Chicken & Onions)

- **Icelandic Skyr with Berries & Honey** (Thick Yogurt)
- **Pakistani Halwa Puri** (Fried Bread with Sweet Semolina)
- **Belgian Liege Waffles** (Sugar-Crusted Yeast Waffles)
- **Cuban Tostada con Café** (Pressed Bread with Butter & Coffee)
- **Nigerian Akara** (Black-Eyed Pea Fritters)
- **Kuwaiti Balaleet** (Sweet Vermicelli with Cardamom & Eggs)
- **Singaporean Kaya Toast with Soft-Boiled Eggs** (Coconut Jam Toast)
- **Ukrainian Deruny** (Potato Pancakes with Sour Cream)
- **Chilean Marraqueta with Avocado** (Crispy Bread with Mashed Avocado)
- **Canadian Maple Bacon Pancakes** (Fluffy Pancakes with Maple Syrup & Bacon)
- **Saudi Arabian Harees** (Slow-Cooked Wheat & Meat Porridge)
- **Venezuelan Cachapas** (Corn Pancakes with Cheese)
- **Romanian Mămăligă cu Brânză** (Polenta with Cheese & Sour Cream)
- **Hawaiian Loco Moco** (Rice with Burger Patty, Gravy & Egg)
- **Burmese Mohinga** (Rice Noodle Soup with Fish Broth)
- **Algerian Msemen** (Layered, Buttered Flatbread)

Japanese Tamago Kake Gohan (Egg Over Rice)

Ingredients:

- 1 cup hot cooked rice
- 1 raw egg
- 1 tsp soy sauce
- 1/2 tsp sesame oil (optional)
- 1 pinch of salt
- 1 tsp chopped green onions (optional)

Instructions:

1. Place hot rice in a bowl.
2. Crack a raw egg over the rice.
3. Drizzle with soy sauce and sesame oil.
4. Stir vigorously until creamy.
5. Garnish with green onions if desired.

French Croissant aux Amandes (Almond Croissant)

Ingredients:

- 4 day-old croissants
- 1/2 cup almond flour
- 1/4 cup sugar
- 1/4 cup unsalted butter, softened
- 1 egg
- 1/2 tsp vanilla extract
- 1/2 tsp almond extract
- 1/4 cup sliced almonds
- Powdered sugar for dusting

Instructions:

1. Preheat oven to 350°F (175°C).
2. Mix almond flour, sugar, butter, egg, vanilla, and almond extract into a paste.
3. Slice croissants open and spread filling inside.
4. Spread a thin layer on top and sprinkle with almonds.
5. Bake for 10–15 minutes until golden.
6. Dust with powdered sugar before serving.

Mexican Chilaquiles con Huevos

Ingredients:

- 4 corn tortillas, cut into triangles
- 1 cup red or green salsa
- 2 eggs
- 1/4 cup crumbled queso fresco
- 1/4 cup sour cream
- 1 tbsp chopped cilantro
- 1 tbsp oil

Instructions:

1. Fry tortilla pieces in oil until crispy.
2. Add salsa and toss to coat.
3. Fry eggs separately and place on top.
4. Garnish with cheese, sour cream, and cilantro.

Turkish Menemen (Spicy Scrambled Eggs with Tomatoes)

Ingredients:

- 3 eggs
- 2 tomatoes, diced
- 1 green bell pepper, chopped
- 1 onion, diced
- 2 tbsp olive oil
- 1 tsp red pepper flakes
- Salt and pepper to taste

Instructions:

1. Heat oil in a pan, sauté onion and pepper until soft.
2. Add tomatoes and cook until softened.
3. Crack eggs into the pan and stir gently until scrambled.
4. Season with red pepper flakes, salt, and pepper.

English Full Breakfast (Bacon, Eggs, Sausages, Beans)

Ingredients:

- 2 slices of bacon
- 2 sausages
- 2 eggs
- 1/2 cup baked beans
- 1 slice of toast
- 1 tomato, halved
- 1/2 cup mushrooms, sliced

Instructions:

1. Fry bacon and sausages until golden.
2. Cook mushrooms and tomato in the same pan.
3. Heat baked beans in a pot.
4. Fry eggs separately.
5. Serve everything with toast.

Indian Masala Dosa (Fermented Rice Crepe with Spiced Potatoes)

Ingredients:

- **For dosa batter:**
    - 1 cup rice
    - 1/2 cup urad dal (split black gram)
    - 1/2 tsp salt
- **For potato filling:**
    - 2 boiled potatoes, mashed
    - 1 onion, sliced
    - 1/2 tsp mustard seeds
    - 1/2 tsp turmeric
    - 1/2 tsp cumin
    - 1 tbsp oil

Instructions:

1. Soak rice and urad dal overnight, then blend into a smooth batter. Let ferment for 6 hours.
2. Heat oil, sauté mustard seeds, cumin, and onion. Add turmeric and mashed potatoes.
3. Pour batter onto a hot griddle, cook until crispy.
4. Fill with potato mixture and fold.

Spanish Tortilla Española (Potato and Egg Omelet)

Ingredients:

- 3 potatoes, peeled and sliced
- 1 onion, sliced
- 4 eggs
- 1/4 cup olive oil
- Salt to taste

Instructions:

1. Heat olive oil in a pan and fry potatoes and onions until soft.
2. Beat eggs and add potatoes.
3. Pour back into the pan and cook until set.
4. Flip and cook the other side.

German Bauernfrühstück (Farmer's Breakfast with Potatoes & Eggs)

Ingredients:

- 2 potatoes, boiled and diced
- 1/2 onion, chopped
- 2 slices bacon, chopped
- 2 eggs
- 1 tbsp butter
- Salt and pepper to taste

Instructions:

1. Fry bacon and onion in butter.
2. Add potatoes and cook until golden.
3. Crack eggs over the potatoes and stir.
4. Season with salt and pepper.

Korean Gyeran Bap (Egg Rice Bowl with Sesame Oil)

Ingredients:

- 1 cup cooked rice
- 1 fried egg
- 1 tsp soy sauce
- 1/2 tsp sesame oil
- 1/2 tsp sesame seeds
- 1 tbsp chopped green onions

Instructions:

1. Place hot rice in a bowl.
2. Top with a fried egg.
3. Drizzle with soy sauce and sesame oil.
4. Garnish with sesame seeds and green onions.

Argentine Medialunas con Dulce de Leche (Sweet Croissants with Caramel)

Ingredients:

- 4 small croissants
- 1/2 cup dulce de leche
- 1 tbsp butter
- 1 tbsp sugar

Instructions:

1. Slice croissants in half and spread dulce de leche inside.
2. Brush tops with butter and sprinkle with sugar.
3. Bake at 350°F (175°C) for 5 minutes until warm.

Lebanese Manakish Za'atar (Flatbread with Thyme & Olive Oil)

Ingredients:

- 2 cups all-purpose flour
- 1 tsp salt
- 1 tsp sugar
- 1 tsp dry yeast
- 3/4 cup warm water
- 1 tbsp olive oil
- **Za'atar topping:**
    - 1/4 cup za'atar spice
    - 1/4 cup olive oil

Instructions:

1. Mix flour, salt, sugar, and yeast in a bowl. Add water and knead until smooth. Let rise for 1 hour.
2. Roll out dough into small circles.
3. Mix za'atar with olive oil and spread over dough.
4. Bake at 400°F (200°C) for 10–12 minutes until golden.

Russian Syrniki (Sweet Cheese Pancakes)

Ingredients:

- 1 cup farmer's cheese or ricotta
- 1 egg
- 1/4 cup flour
- 2 tbsp sugar
- 1/2 tsp vanilla extract
- 1 tbsp butter (for frying)
- Powdered sugar and jam for serving

Instructions:

1. Mix cheese, egg, flour, sugar, and vanilla until combined.
2. Shape into small pancakes and coat lightly in flour.
3. Fry in butter over medium heat until golden on both sides.
4. Serve with powdered sugar and jam.

Chinese Dim Sum Breakfast (Variety of Steamed Dumplings)

Ingredients:

- 1 pack dumpling wrappers
- **Filling:**
    - 1/2 lb ground pork or shrimp
    - 2 tbsp soy sauce
    - 1 tsp sesame oil
    - 1 tbsp chopped green onions
    - 1/2 tsp ginger, grated

Instructions:

1. Mix filling ingredients.
2. Place small spoonfuls into wrappers, fold and seal.
3. Steam dumplings for 10 minutes until cooked through.
4. Serve with soy sauce or chili oil.

Brazilian Pão de Queijo (Cheese Bread)

Ingredients:

- 2 cups tapioca flour
- 1/2 cup milk
- 1/4 cup butter
- 1 egg
- 1 cup grated Parmesan cheese
- 1/2 tsp salt

Instructions:

1. Preheat oven to 375°F (190°C).
2. Heat milk and butter until warm. Mix with tapioca flour.
3. Add egg, cheese, and salt. Stir into a sticky dough.
4. Shape into balls and bake for 20 minutes until golden.

Moroccan Bissara (Fava Bean Soup with Olive Oil)

Ingredients:

- 1 cup dried fava beans, soaked
- 3 cups water
- 2 cloves garlic, minced
- 1 tsp cumin
- 1/2 tsp paprika
- 1 tbsp olive oil

Instructions:

1. Boil fava beans in water until soft (about 30 minutes).
2. Blend into a smooth soup.
3. Stir in garlic, cumin, paprika, and salt.
4. Drizzle with olive oil before serving.

Italian Cornetto e Cappuccino (Pastry with Coffee)

Ingredients:

- 4 store-bought or homemade cornetti (Italian croissants)
- 1/2 cup pastry cream or jam
- 2 cups hot milk
- 2 shots espresso

Instructions:

1. Slice cornetti and fill with pastry cream or jam.
2. Froth milk and mix with espresso for a cappuccino.
3. Serve together for an Italian breakfast.

Vietnamese Bánh Mì Op La (Egg and Baguette Sandwich)

Ingredients:

- 1 baguette, halved
- 2 eggs
- 1 tbsp butter
- 1/4 cucumber, sliced
- 1/4 cup pickled carrots and daikon
- 1 tbsp soy sauce
- 1 tbsp cilantro

Instructions:

1. Fry eggs in butter until crispy on the edges.
2. Place eggs inside baguette with cucumbers, pickled vegetables, and cilantro.
3. Drizzle with soy sauce before serving.

Dutch Poffertjes (Mini Pancakes with Butter & Powdered Sugar)

Ingredients:

- 1 cup flour
- 1/2 cup milk
- 1 egg
- 1/2 tsp yeast
- 1 tbsp sugar
- 1 tbsp butter (for frying)
- Powdered sugar for serving

Instructions:

1. Mix flour, yeast, sugar, milk, and egg into a batter. Let rest for 30 minutes.
2. Cook small spoonfuls in a poffertjes pan or skillet.
3. Serve with butter and powdered sugar.

Filipino Tapsilog (Beef, Garlic Rice & Fried Egg)

Ingredients:

- 1/2 lb beef sirloin, thinly sliced
- 2 tbsp soy sauce
- 1 tbsp vinegar
- 2 cloves garlic, minced
- 1 cup cooked rice
- 1 egg
- 1 tbsp oil

Instructions:

1. Marinate beef in soy sauce, vinegar, and garlic for 30 minutes.
2. Sauté beef until browned.
3. Fry rice with garlic and cook egg separately.
4. Serve everything together.

Swedish Gravlax Smörgås (Cured Salmon on Dark Rye Bread)

Ingredients:

- 4 slices dark rye bread
- 4 oz gravlax (cured salmon)
- 2 tbsp cream cheese
- 1 tbsp fresh dill, chopped
- 1 tsp lemon juice

Instructions:

1. Spread cream cheese on rye bread.
2. Top with gravlax, dill, and lemon juice.
3. Serve open-faced.

Greek Bougatsa (Custard-Filled Pastry with Cinnamon)

Ingredients:

- 6 sheets phyllo dough
- 2 cups milk
- 1/2 cup sugar
- 1/4 cup semolina flour
- 2 eggs
- 1 tsp vanilla extract
- 4 tbsp butter, melted
- Powdered sugar and cinnamon for garnish

Instructions:

1. Heat milk and sugar, then whisk in semolina. Cook until thickened.
2. Remove from heat, beat in eggs and vanilla.
3. Brush phyllo sheets with butter, layering them in a baking dish.
4. Spread custard filling, fold phyllo over, and bake at 375°F (190°C) for 30 minutes.
5. Dust with powdered sugar and cinnamon before serving.

South African Boerewors and Pap (Sausage with Maize Porridge)

Ingredients:

- 1 lb boerewors sausage
- 1 cup maize meal (cornmeal)
- 3 cups water
- 1/2 tsp salt
- 1 tbsp butter

Instructions:

1. Grill boerewors until browned.
2. Bring water to a boil, stir in maize meal and salt. Cook for 10 minutes, stirring.
3. Add butter and serve with sausage.

Ethiopian Genfo (Barley Porridge with Spiced Butter)

Ingredients:

- 1 cup barley flour
- 2 cups water
- 1/2 tsp salt
- 2 tbsp spiced butter (niter kibbeh)
- 1 tsp berbere spice

Instructions:

1. Boil water, then slowly whisk in barley flour and salt.
2. Stir continuously until thick.
3. Serve with melted spiced butter and berbere on top.

Persian Kuku Sabzi (Herb and Egg Frittata)

Ingredients:

- 1 cup chopped parsley
- 1/2 cup chopped cilantro
- 1/2 cup chopped dill
- 4 eggs
- 1/2 tsp turmeric
- 1/2 tsp salt
- 1 tbsp olive oil

Instructions:

1. Whisk eggs with turmeric and salt, then mix in herbs.
2. Heat oil in a pan, pour in mixture, and cook until set.
3. Flip and cook the other side.

Austrian Kaiserschmarrn (Caramelized Pancake with Raisins)

Ingredients:

- 1 cup flour
- 1 cup milk
- 2 eggs, separated
- 2 tbsp sugar
- 1/4 cup raisins
- 1 tbsp butter
- Powdered sugar for topping

Instructions:

1. Whisk flour, milk, and egg yolks. Beat egg whites and fold in.
2. Cook batter in butter over medium heat.
3. Add raisins, break pancake into pieces, and caramelize with sugar.
4. Serve with powdered sugar.

Thai Jok (Rice Porridge with Pork and Ginger)

Ingredients:

- 1/2 cup jasmine rice
- 4 cups chicken broth
- 1/2 lb ground pork
- 1 tsp fish sauce
- 1 tsp grated ginger
- 1 egg (optional)
- Chopped green onions for garnish

Instructions:

1. Simmer rice in broth until soft.
2. Mix pork with fish sauce and ginger, then drop small pieces into the porridge.
3. Cook until pork is done.
4. Top with an egg (if desired) and green onions.

Colombian Arepas con Queso (Cheese-Stuffed Corn Cakes)

Ingredients:

- 1 cup masa harina (corn flour)
- 1/2 cup warm water
- 1/2 cup shredded cheese
- 1/2 tsp salt
- 1 tbsp butter

Instructions:

1. Mix masa, water, salt, and cheese into a dough.
2. Shape into discs and cook in a buttered pan until golden.

Danish Wienerbrød (Layered Pastry with Almond Paste)

Ingredients:

- 1 sheet puff pastry
- 1/2 cup almond paste
- 2 tbsp sugar
- 1 egg, beaten
- Sliced almonds for garnish

Instructions:

1. Roll out pastry and spread almond paste mixed with sugar.
2. Fold over, cut into shapes, and brush with egg wash.
3. Bake at 375°F (190°C) for 15–20 minutes.

Polish Racuchy (Yeast Pancakes with Apples)

Ingredients:

- 1 cup flour
- 1/2 cup milk
- 1 tsp yeast
- 1 tbsp sugar
- 1 apple, grated
- 1 egg
- 1/2 tsp cinnamon

Instructions:

1. Mix flour, milk, yeast, and sugar. Let rise for 30 minutes.
2. Stir in apple, egg, and cinnamon.
3. Fry small pancakes until golden.

Hungarian Lángos (Fried Dough with Sour Cream & Cheese)

Ingredients:

- 2 cups flour
- 1/2 cup warm milk
- 1 tsp yeast
- 1/2 tsp salt
- 1 tbsp oil
- 1/2 cup sour cream
- 1/2 cup shredded cheese

Instructions:

1. Mix flour, milk, yeast, and salt into a dough. Let rise for 1 hour.
2. Roll out and fry in hot oil.
3. Top with sour cream and cheese.

Finnish Karjalanpiirakka (Rice-Filled Rye Pastry)

Ingredients:

- **Dough:**
    - 1 cup rye flour
    - 1/2 cup all-purpose flour
    - 1/2 cup water
    - 1/2 tsp salt
- **Filling:**
    - 1 cup cooked rice porridge
    - 1/2 cup milk
    - 1/2 tsp salt

Instructions:

1. Mix dough ingredients and roll out into thin ovals.
2. Fill with rice mixture and crimp edges.
3. Bake at 400°F (200°C) for 15 minutes.

Indonesian Bubur Ayam (Chicken Rice Porridge)

Ingredients:

- 1/2 cup jasmine rice
- 4 cups chicken broth
- 1/2 cup shredded chicken
- 1 boiled egg, sliced
- 1 tbsp fried shallots
- 1 tbsp chopped green onions
- 1 tsp soy sauce
- 1 tsp fried peanuts
- 1/2 tsp white pepper

Instructions:

1. Simmer rice in chicken broth until thick and creamy.
2. Stir in shredded chicken and season with soy sauce.
3. Garnish with egg, shallots, green onions, peanuts, and pepper.

Egyptian Ful Medames (Slow-Cooked Fava Beans with Garlic)

Ingredients:

- 1 cup dried fava beans, soaked overnight
- 3 cups water
- 2 cloves garlic, minced
- 2 tbsp olive oil
- 1 tbsp lemon juice
- 1/2 tsp cumin
- 1 tbsp chopped parsley

Instructions:

1. Simmer fava beans in water until soft (about 1 hour).
2. Mash beans slightly, then stir in garlic, olive oil, lemon juice, and cumin.
3. Garnish with parsley before serving.

Peruvian Tamal con Salsa Criolla (Corn Dough with Chicken & Onions)

Ingredients:

- **For tamales:**
    - 2 cups masa harina (corn flour)
    - 1/2 cup chicken broth
    - 1/2 cup shredded chicken
    - 1 tsp cumin
    - 1/2 tsp salt
    - Banana leaves (for wrapping)
- **For salsa criolla:**
    - 1 red onion, thinly sliced
    - 1 tbsp lime juice
    - 1/2 tsp salt
    - 1/2 tsp chopped cilantro

Instructions:

1. Mix masa harina, broth, chicken, cumin, and salt into a dough.
2. Place dough in banana leaves, fold, and steam for 40 minutes.
3. Toss onions with lime juice, salt, and cilantro for salsa.
4. Serve tamales with salsa criolla on top.

Icelandic Skyr with Berries & Honey (Thick Yogurt)

Ingredients:

- 1 cup skyr (Icelandic yogurt)
- 1/4 cup mixed berries
- 1 tbsp honey
- 1 tbsp chopped nuts (optional)

Instructions:

1. Spoon skyr into a bowl.
2. Top with berries, drizzle with honey, and add nuts if desired.

Pakistani Halwa Puri (Fried Bread with Sweet Semolina)

Ingredients:

- **For puri:**
    - 1 cup flour
    - 1/4 tsp salt
    - 1/4 cup water
    - Oil for frying
- **For halwa:**
    - 1/2 cup semolina (sooji)
    - 1/4 cup sugar
    - 1/4 cup ghee
    - 1/2 tsp cardamom
    - 1/2 cup water

Instructions:

1. Mix flour, salt, and water into dough, roll out small discs, and fry until puffed.
2. In a pan, cook semolina in ghee until golden.
3. Add sugar, cardamom, and water, stirring until thick.
4. Serve puri with warm halwa.

Belgian Liège Waffles (Sugar-Crusted Yeast Waffles)

Ingredients:

- 2 cups flour
- 1/2 cup warm milk
- 2 tbsp sugar
- 1 tsp yeast
- 1/2 cup pearl sugar
- 1/2 cup melted butter
- 1 egg

Instructions:

1. Mix warm milk, yeast, and sugar. Let sit for 5 minutes.
2. Stir in flour, egg, and melted butter. Let rise for 1 hour.
3. Fold in pearl sugar, then cook in a waffle iron until golden.

Cuban Tostada con Café (Pressed Bread with Butter & Coffee)

Ingredients:

- 2 slices Cuban bread
- 2 tbsp butter
- 1 shot espresso
- 1/2 cup steamed milk

Instructions:

1. Butter Cuban bread and press it in a pan until golden.
2. Brew espresso and mix with steamed milk.
3. Serve together for dipping.

Nigerian Akara (Black-Eyed Pea Fritters)

Ingredients:

- 1 cup black-eyed peas, soaked and peeled
- 1/2 onion, chopped
- 1/2 tsp cayenne pepper
- 1/2 tsp salt
- 1 cup oil (for frying)

Instructions:

1. Blend peas, onion, cayenne, and salt into a thick batter.
2. Heat oil and drop spoonfuls of batter, frying until golden.

Kuwaiti Balaleet (Sweet Vermicelli with Cardamom & Eggs)

Ingredients:

- 1 cup vermicelli noodles
- 2 tbsp sugar
- 1/2 tsp ground cardamom
- 1/2 tsp saffron
- 1 tbsp butter
- 2 eggs, scrambled

Instructions:

1. Cook vermicelli in boiling water, then drain.
2. Melt butter in a pan, add noodles, sugar, cardamom, and saffron.
3. Top with scrambled eggs.

Singaporean Kaya Toast with Soft-Boiled Eggs (Coconut Jam Toast)

Ingredients:

- 2 slices white bread
- 2 tbsp kaya (coconut jam)
- 1 tbsp butter
- 2 eggs
- 1 tsp soy sauce

Instructions:

1. Toast bread and spread kaya and butter.
2. Soft-boil eggs for 6 minutes, then serve with soy sauce.
3. Dip kaya toast into eggs before eating.

Ukrainian Deruny (Potato Pancakes with Sour Cream)

Ingredients:

- 4 potatoes, grated
- 1 small onion, grated
- 1 egg
- 2 tbsp flour
- 1/2 tsp salt
- 1/4 tsp black pepper
- 2 tbsp vegetable oil (for frying)
- Sour cream for serving

Instructions:

1. Mix grated potatoes, onion, egg, flour, salt, and pepper.
2. Heat oil in a pan, drop spoonfuls of batter, and flatten.
3. Fry until golden brown on both sides.
4. Serve with sour cream.

Chilean Marraqueta with Avocado (Crispy Bread with Mashed Avocado)

Ingredients:

- 2 marraqueta rolls (or crusty bread)
- 1 ripe avocado
- 1 tsp olive oil
- 1/2 tsp salt
- 1/4 tsp black pepper

Instructions:

1. Toast marraqueta rolls.
2. Mash avocado with olive oil, salt, and pepper.
3. Spread avocado on toasted bread.

Canadian Maple Bacon Pancakes (Fluffy Pancakes with Maple Syrup & Bacon)

Ingredients:

- 1 cup flour
- 1 tbsp sugar
- 1 tsp baking powder
- 1/2 tsp salt
- 3/4 cup milk
- 1 egg
- 2 tbsp melted butter
- 4 strips crispy bacon, crumbled
- Maple syrup for serving

Instructions:

1. Mix flour, sugar, baking powder, and salt.
2. Whisk in milk, egg, and butter.
3. Fold in crumbled bacon.
4. Cook pancakes on a skillet until golden brown.
5. Serve with maple syrup.

Saudi Arabian Harees (Slow-Cooked Wheat & Meat Porridge)

Ingredients:

- 1 cup whole wheat berries (soaked overnight)
- 1 lb lamb or chicken, cubed
- 6 cups water
- 1 tsp salt
- 1/2 tsp cinnamon
- 2 tbsp butter

Instructions:

1. Simmer wheat and meat in water for 2–3 hours, stirring occasionally.
2. Blend or mash until smooth.
3. Stir in salt, cinnamon, and butter before serving.

Venezuelan Cachapas (Corn Pancakes with Cheese)

Ingredients:

- 2 cups corn kernels (fresh or canned)
- 1/2 cup milk
- 1/2 cup cornmeal
- 1 tbsp sugar
- 1/2 tsp salt
- 1 tbsp butter
- 1/2 cup queso fresco or mozzarella

Instructions:

1. Blend corn, milk, cornmeal, sugar, and salt into a batter.
2. Cook pancakes on a buttered skillet until golden.
3. Fill with cheese and fold.

Romanian Mămăligă cu Brânză (Polenta with Cheese & Sour Cream)

Ingredients:

- 1 cup cornmeal
- 3 cups water
- 1/2 tsp salt
- 1/2 cup feta cheese, crumbled
- 1/4 cup sour cream
- 1 tbsp butter

Instructions:

1. Boil water, stir in cornmeal and salt, and cook until thick.
2. Stir in butter, then top with feta and sour cream.

Hawaiian Loco Moco (Rice with Burger Patty, Gravy & Egg)

Ingredients:

- 1 cup cooked rice
- 1 beef patty
- 1/2 cup beef broth
- 1 tsp cornstarch (mixed with 1 tbsp water)
- 1 egg
- 1 tbsp butter

Instructions:

1. Cook beef patty in a pan.
2. Make gravy by whisking cornstarch into beef broth, simmering until thick.
3. Fry egg in butter.
4. Serve beef patty over rice, topped with gravy and egg.

Burmese Mohinga (Rice Noodle Soup with Fish Broth)

Ingredients:

- 1/2 lb catfish or white fish, cooked and flaked
- 4 cups fish broth
- 1/2 cup rice noodles
- 1 tbsp fish sauce
- 1/2 tsp turmeric
- 1 garlic clove, minced
- 1/2 tsp ginger, grated
- 1/2 cup chopped cilantro

Instructions:

1. Simmer fish broth with fish sauce, turmeric, garlic, and ginger.
2. Add rice noodles and cook until tender.
3. Stir in flaked fish and garnish with cilantro.

Algerian Msemen (Layered, Buttered Flatbread)

Ingredients:

- 2 cups flour
- 1 cup semolina flour
- 1/2 tsp salt
- 3/4 cup warm water
- 1/4 cup butter, melted
- 1/4 cup vegetable oil

Instructions:

1. Mix flour, semolina, salt, and water into a dough. Let rest for 30 minutes.
2. Roll out thin, brush with butter and oil, fold into a square, and flatten.
3. Cook on a hot skillet until golden brown on both sides.

www.ingramcontent.com/pod-product-compliance
Lightning Source LLC
LaVergne TN
LVHW081500060526
838201LV00056BA/2842